IN MEMORY OF JOHNATHON

© 2024 by Amy Parker
All Rights Reserved

Published in 2024 by
Walking Together Press
Estes Park, Colorado USA
Jenta Mangoro, Jos, Plateau Nigeria
walkingtogether.press

ISBN: 978-1-961568-75-4

Unless otherwise noted, all Scripture quotations are taken from the Holman Christian Standard Bible®, Copyright © 1999, 2000, 2002, 2003, 2009 by Holman Bible Publishers. Used by permission. Holman Christian Standard Bible®, Holman CSB®, and HCSB® are federally registered trademarks of Holman Bible Publishers.

Scripture quotations marked NASB are taken from the New American Standard Bible®, Copyright © 1960, 1962, 1963, 1968, 1971, 1972, 1973, 1975, 1977, 1995 by the Lockman Foundation. Used by permission. (www.lockman.org).

Scripture quotations noted as NCV are taken from the New Century Version®. Copyright © 2005 by Thomas Nelson. Used by permission. All rights reserved. Scripture quotations marked NIV are taken from the Holy Bible, NEW INTERNATIONAL VERSION®. Copyright © 1973, 1978, 1984 by Biblica, Inc. All rights reserved worldwide. Used by permission.

Book and cover design by: Jacoba Looije

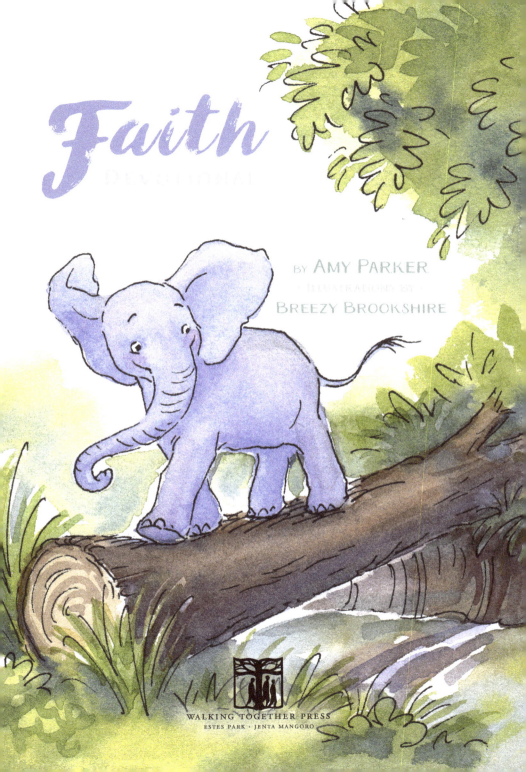

Faith
Devotional

BY AMY PARKER
ILLUSTRATIONS BY
BREEZY BROOKSHIRE

WALKING TOGETHER PRESS
ESTES PARK · JENTA MANGORO

Contents

Faith is 2
Seeing the Invisible 4
Not by Sight 6
Noah's Faith 8
Abraham's Faith 10
The Israelites' Faith 12
Pleasing to God 14
Rewarding to Us 16
Faith Is Strong 18
Find the Faithful 20
Faithful Steps 22
Above All 24
Friends of Faith 26
More Than Most 28
Set Apart 30
Love the Lord 32
Never Alone 34

A Faithful Hero	36
Written on Your Heart	38
God's Delight	40
Blessed	42
Stand Firm	44
Live by Faith	46
Fearless	48
Faith You Can See	50
"Why did you Doubt?"	52
Mustard-Seed Faith	54
Faithful over a Few	56
Grow Our Faith	68
Forgiveness by Faith	60
Stand by Faith	62
Victory!	64
Faith and Hope	66

Faith is...

Now faith is . . . the proof of what is not seen.

—Hebrews 11:1

*F*aith. It's a word you may hear a lot. It may even be a word you use a lot.

> "I have faith in you."
>
> "Take a leap of faith!"
>
> "A dog is a faithful friend."

But have you ever really tried to tell someone what it means? Hmm. That's a tough one. And when the going gets tough, the tough open their Bibles.

Hebrews 11 describes faith as "the proof of what is not seen." Like feeling the unseen wind on your face, faith is a feeling in your heart that just knows. God has told us about Himself, and we can trust what He has said. You know God created the universe. You *believe* He is always with you. God has no limits and is always everywhere. You trust that He is always listening. He is in control of everything. That knowing, that believing, that trusting is faith.

It grows over time with every little whisper from God. Every rainbow, every kiss on the forehead, and every answered prayer are all proof of God and the promises that He has for us.

Believe, trust, know . . . and your faith will continue to grow.

 **Tell me about it**

In your own words, what is faith?

 **Think about it**

What are some ways that God has whispered His love to you? How do you know He's there?

 DO IT!

Go out—today—and tell someone what *faith* means to you!

Seeing the Invisible

By faith we understand that the universe was created by God's command, so that what is seen has been made from things that are not visible.

—Hebrews 11:3

The very first sentence of the Bible says, "In the beginning God created the heavens and the earth" (Genesis 1:1). And that beginning is a perfect place to start building our faith.

When your faith feels weak and you wish you could actually see God, you can look around and *know*. Know that these amazing things that you can see and smell and touch—like mountains and monkeys and maple trees—came from "things that are not visible." The entire world came to be when your almighty Creator, your Savior, your God simply spoke.

When you start there, when you look around and know that the very first sentence in the Bible is true, it reminds you that the rest of His Word is too. When you read about God and His creation and His people, you *know*, you believe, you feel that it's real.

That, my friend, is faith. And see? Yours is already beginning to grow.

📣 Tell me about it

What is one thing God created that completely amazes you?

💡 Think about it

Now, go back to creation, and imagine that one thing being made. Can you picture God creating it out of nothing?

✋ DO IT!

Spend some time learning all you can about that one thing, and be amazed by what God can create by simply speaking a word.

Not by Sight

For we walk by faith, not by sight.
—2 Corinthians 5:7

We *can* look out at all that God created and know that He is there. But true faith is believing even though you can't see. As we spend time with God and grow closer to Him, we will have all the proof we need. (Remember Hebrews 11:1?)

Thomas, a disciple of Jesus, knew that Jesus had died on the cross. But when Thomas heard that Jesus was alive again, he said, "If I don't see the mark of the nails in His hands, . . . I will never believe!" (John 20:25). And who could blame him? It was quite a story!

Then Jesus Himself went to Thomas and showed him the marks in His hands. And Thomas believed. Jesus told Thomas, "Because you have seen Me, you have believed. Those who believe without seeing are blessed" (John 20:29).

Jesus can prove Himself to you. But let's be blessed by believing without seeing!

📣 Tell me about it
What is one thing about Jesus that you think is hard to believe?

💡 Think about it
Think about all the things you know about God that are true. Why is this one thing different?

✋ DO IT!
Talk to God now and ask Him to help you believe without seeing.

Noah's Faith

By faith Noah, after he was warned about what was not yet seen and motivated by godly fear, built an ark to deliver his family.

—Hebrews 11:7

After Hebrews 11 explains faith, it gives us a lot of examples of faith heroes in the Bible. And Noah was definitely one of them.

Talk about believing in the unseen! God told Noah to build a huge boat with supplies he didn't have for a flood that wouldn't happen for years and years. And Noah listened!

God gave him exact details: "Use cypress wood. Build it this tall, this wide, and this high. Put the door here. Coat it with tar." And Noah obeyed every word.

In a world full of evil people who have turned away from God, Noah believed.

Noah obeyed. Noah had faith. And as a result, his entire family was saved.

 **Tell me about it**

What are some ways that you obey God?

 Think about it

How could you be more like Noah in your obedience and faith?

 DO IT!

Read (or ask someone to read to you) the whole story of Noah in Genesis 6–9.

Do you ever wonder when God's promises are going to come true for *you*? I'm sure Abraham wondered the same thing.

God had promised to make Abraham "into a great nation" (Genesis 12:2), but Abraham spent much of his life living in a tent. God had promised Abraham that he would be the father of many people, as many as the stars in the sky (15:5). But at that moment, Abraham was the father of *no one*.

Still, Abraham held tight to the promises of God and followed where He led. Abraham knew that God would make His promises come true, no matter how difficult they seemed. And you know what? That's exactly what happened. Through Abraham, the Israelites (God's chosen people) became a great nation with as many people as the stars in the sky.

It can be hard to keep the faith when you don't see God's promises shining all around you. But hang in there. Keep following Him and holding tight to His promises. They will always be true.

📣 Tell me about it
What are some promises that God has made to you? (See Deuteronomy 4:29; Philippians 4:19; Jeremiah 29:11; or 1 John 1:9 for starters.)

💡 Think about it
If God can create a great nation out of Abraham, imagine what He can do with you!

✋ DO IT!
On the next clear night, try to count the stars in the sky just as God asked Abraham to do.

The Israelites had just left the only home they'd ever known. They were carrying everything they owned on their backs, pushing carts, pulling sheep. It was a loud, confusing mass of people and animals and stuff. But God's promise to set them free, to make them a great nation, was coming true. They were leaving the harsh rule of the Egyptians, headed to the home God had promised them.

Suddenly, the crowd halted. They had reached the edge of the Red Sea and could go no farther. But behind them, the Egyptian soldiers were coming. Fast. And they were *not* happy. Fear erupted in the crowd. But Moses looked to the Lord.

As Moses stretched his hand out over the sea, God sent a powerful wind that split the water in two, leaving a dry path for His people to walk through.

Would they make it safely *across*? And where was *across* anyway? They didn't know, but they knew that God was leading the way. So one by one, the people walked by faith through the middle of the Red Sea and into God's promises for them.

📢 Tell me about it

Name a time when God has brought you safely through something that scared you.

💡 Think about it

Imagine standing there, on a dry path in the middle of the Red Sea. What would you see, smell, feel?

✋ DO IT!

Take a moment to thank God for His constant protection, wherever He may lead.

Pleasing to God

Now without faith it is impossible to please God.

—Hebrews 11:6

Noah. Abraham. The Israelites. These faith heroes all had big roles in God's perfect plan.

But what would have happened if Noah hadn't built that boat?

Or if Abraham had given up on God's promise?

Or if the Israelites had never crossed that Red Sea?

We can't know for sure. But we do know this: because of their great faith, Noah, Abraham, and the Israelites pleased God and were able to play a big part in His plan.

Without faith, it's impossible. But with *faith*, well, you just never know where you may go.

 **Tell me about it**
How did Noah, Abraham, and the Israelites please God?

 Think about it
How can you play a part in God's plan?

 DO IT!
Do one thing today to step out in big faith!

Rewarding to Us

The one who draws near to Him must believe that He exists and rewards those who seek Him.

—Hebrews 11:6

Just as our faith pleases God, it can also bring big rewards. No, you probably won't get a trophy or even an ice cream cone. God's rewards are actually much bigger than that.

You may find His rewards in the warmth of a sunshiny day or the smile of a friend. But we could never count or measure the rewards given to those who seek, learn about, and become closer to God throughout their lives. The lasting reward of a faith-filled life stretches all the way into eternity.

A life of seeking (looking for) God will not always be easy. But it will always be the most rewarding way to live—both here on earth and in heaven.

: Tell me about it

Name one way that you can seek God daily.

Think about it

How did God reward Noah, Abraham, or the Israelites for their faithfulness?

DO IT!

Create a medal for yourself with the words "Seek Him," to always remind you of the life God rewards.

Faith Is Strong

By faith the walls of Jericho fell down after being encircled by the Israelites for seven days.

—Hebrews 11:30

Even for the faithful, sometimes God's plans seem plain silly. Just ask Joshua.

When Moses died, God chose Joshua to lead the Israelites into their promised land. The first stop was Jericho, a big city that God had given to the Israelites. But there was only one problem: there was a humongous wall around Jericho.

So God told Joshua how to get in. "Look, I've already given the city to you. March around the city one time for six days. Then on the seventh day, go around seven times, have the priests blow the trumpets, and tell the people to shout. Then the wall will fall" (see Joshua 6:1–5).

Wait . . . *what?* No bulldozers? No battering rams?

Nope. Just faith in the mighty hand of God.

And you know what? The Israelites marched—one round for six days, seven rounds on the seventh. Then, when those trumpets blasted and the people shouted, the walls came crumbling down.

Hmm. So maybe we should follow God's instructions, whether they make sense to us or not. And when we do, the walls just may fall, clearing the way to all of God's promises for us.

📢 Tell me about it
How did Joshua react to God's directions?

💡 Think about it
What are some directions God gives you?

✋ DO IT!
Spend your day trying to listen to and follow God's directions to you. Then tomorrow, try it again! And the next day, and the next . . .

Find the Faithful

And what more can I say? Time is too short for me to tell about Gideon, Barak, Samson, Jephthan, David, Samuel, and the prophets.

—Hebrews 11:32

By Hebrews 11:32, the writer's hand must have been getting tired. "What more can I say?" he asked. He had told us about the faith of Abel and Enoch and Noah and Abraham and Sarah and Isaac and Jacob and didn't have time for Gideon, Barak, Samson, Jephthah, David . . . Whew! Now *my* hand is getting tired!

There are so many examples of obedient, faithful people in the Bible. There are so many heroes to look up to and to guide us when we need help. But you know what? Those people are all around us too. Our parents and teachers and maybe even that big brother can help guide us through this walk with God.

So when your faith needs a boost, look to those faithful people around you for support. And remember Abel and Enoch and Noah and Abraham and . . . well, you get the picture. God has surrounded us with all we need in this walk of faith; we'll never have to walk alone.

Tell me about it
Who is your favorite faith hero in the Bible? Why?

Think about it
What could you do to be a faith hero too?

DO IT!
Know someone else who could use a faith boost? Give him or her one today!

Faithful Steps

He guards the steps of His faithful ones.

—1 Samuel 2:9

All of those faithful Bible heroes and all of the faithful people around you—they all have one thing in common. God guards their steps. And He will do the same for you.

Don't you love the way 1 Samuel 2:9 says, "His faithful ones"? Those who are *His* are faithful. He calls us His own. We are precious treasures of the Creator of the universe. And He guards our every step.

When you're a little afraid of where God is leading, when you're feeling unsure about that next step, remember to be faithful. He has promised to protect you, guarding each step as you go.

Tell me about it
Name one person from the Bible whom God protected. How did He protect him or her?

Think about it
How does God protect you?

DO IT!
Trace the outline of your foot, and write 1 Samuel 2:9 on it. Keep it as a reminder that God guards your steps.

Above All

Above all, fear the Lord and worship Him faithfully with all your heart.

—1 Samuel 12:24

What do you love more than anything? Baseball? Bubble gum? Barbie dolls?

Okay, okay, that's kind of a trick question. First Samuel 12:24 tells us that "above all" we should worship God faithfully. To be honest, few of us could say that we truly put God first. We get caught up in school and games and friends, and we sometimes forget that the Creator of the universe is watching over us and waiting to hear from us.

I get it. It's hard to put something first when we don't see it in front of us all the time. And it's hard to worship someone we don't know a whole lot about, right? That's why it's so important to spend time with God every day, to get to know Him, to talk to Him, to read His Word. And the more you learn about Him, the more you hear from Him, the more you'll *want* to worship Him and put Him absolutely first.

After all, He created us. He gave His only Son for us. Placing Him "above all" is the very least we can do.

📢 Tell me about it
It's okay. Be honest. Right now, what do you put first?

💡 Think about it
Why should God come absolutely first?

🙌 DO IT!
What is one way you could put God first today? Do it. Today and every day.

Friends of Faith

Then Saul's son Jonathan came to David in Horesh and encouraged him in his faith in God.

—Samuel 23:16

Do you have a friend who's always smiling . . . who tells you the favorite thing she learned at church that week . . . who treats others the way Jesus would? We all need friends to encourage us in our faith.

David and Jonathan were friends like that. The Bible says that Jonathan loved David "as much as he loved himself" (1 Samuel 18:1). And when David was running scared, in fear for his life, Jonathan found him and reminded him of God's promise to protect him. Jonathan's encouragement kept David going strong.

David and Jonathan were friends of faith, a friendship given and created by God. That is exactly the kind of friends we need. And that's exactly the kind of friend we each need to be.

📣 Tell me about it

Name one friend who encourages you in your faith.

💡 Think about it

How can you cheer others on as they learn more about God?

✋ DO IT!

Make cards with your favorite Bible verses on them. Give the cards to your friends to encourage their faith!

More Than Most

Then I put my brother Hanani in charge of Jerusalem . . . because he was a faithful man who feared God more than most.

—Nehemiah 7:2

When Nehemiah was looking for someone to take charge of the city of Jerusalem, he chose his brother. He didn't choose him because he was big or strong or handsome. He didn't even choose him because he was his brother. Nehemiah chose Hanani because "he was a faithful man."

When people look at you, do they see your faith? First Timothy 4:12 tells us that even young people "should be an example to the believers in speech, in conduct, in love, in faith, in purity." So always remember that the way you act, the way you talk, and the way you believe should be a good example to everyone—even the grown-ups.

 Tell me about it
What are some words people might use to describe you?

Think about it
What are some ways you can show your faith?

DO IT!
Write the letters of your name straight down in a column. Now use one word that starts with each of those letters to describe yourself.

Set Apart

Know that the Lord has set apart the faithful for Himself.

—Psalm 4:3

Let's imagine that there are two lines. In the first line are the people God has set apart for Himself. In the second line is everybody else. Which line would you want to be in?

I don't know about you, but I'm picking the God line. Still, to be in that line, I've got to be faithful. I need to believe in God and His Word and be obedient to them both.

With the choices we make and the actions we take, we are choosing which line we want to stand in. Choose the line of faithful people, the ones set apart for God.

📢 Tell me about it
What do you think it means to be "set apart" for God?

💡 Think about it
How can you choose to be one of the faithful?

✋ DO IT!
Every time you make a decision today, stop and ask if it's the right choice, the one that sets you apart for God. Make the choices of the faithful, knowing that you are set apart for God.

Love the Lord

Love the Lord, all His faithful ones.
　　—Psalm 31:23

How do you show love to your family? Do you spend time with them? Talk with them? Listen to them?

Psalm 31:23 reminds the faithful ones—you and me—to love the Lord too. How exactly can we show our love for the Lord? Well, we can spend time with Him, talk to Him, and listen to Him, like we do with our family. But Jesus tells us another way to show our love: "If you love Me, you will keep My commands" (John 14:15).

It can be hard to follow all of God's commands all the time, but God knows our hearts. He knows when we're trying to do what's right and keep His commands. And when we do, it's one way we can love the Lord.

Loving the Lord is just what we "faithful ones" do. Let's try to do it the way He asks us to.

 Tell me about it
How does God show His love for you?

Think about it
Why do you think it's important that we show our love for Him?

DO IT!
Sing a song. Say a prayer. Obey a command. Find some ways to show God how much you love Him today.

No matter how much we love God, He will always love us more. One way He loves us is by always being with us. Psalm 37:28 tells us that God "will not abandon His faithful ones." He will never leave us alone.

Wherever we are and whatever we're doing, God is always there. He's always watching. He's always listening. And He's always loving us, His faithful ones. It's just one of the many ways He rewards the faithful. (Remember Hebrews 11:6?)

So when you feel afraid or lonely, remember that He is there. He will not leave you.

📣 Tell me about it

Was there ever a time when you felt all alone? What happened?

💡 Think about it

If you had known God was listening at that time, what would you have said to Him?

✋ DO IT!

Draw a picture of the time when you felt alone. Write the words of Psalm 37:28 across the bottom as a reminder that He is always there.

A Faithful Hero

The Lord is faithful in all His words and gracious in all His actions.

—Psalm 145:13

There's no way to get around it: people just aren't perfect. We mess up. We say mean things. And we hurt people's feelings.

Isn't it so nice to know that God is nothing like that? He *is* perfect. He doesn't mess up. And He doesn't make mistakes. He is "faithful" and "gracious in all His actions."

He will never lead us the wrong way. He will never go back on His Word. And He loves us more than we could ever imagine.

So when your heroes let you down, when the world seems scary and mean, put your faith in the one, true Hero: God. He will never let you down.

📣 Tell me about it
Who are some of your heroes?

💡 Think about it
Has a hero ever let you down? How did that make you feel?

✋ DO IT!
Draw a picture of your perfect superhero. And remember the Hero who is always by your side.

Written on Your Heart

Never let loyalty and faithfulness leave you. Tie them around your neck; write them on the tablet of your heart.

—Proverbs 3:3

Having faith everywhere you go, all the time, is tough.

People won't always agree with it. They won't always understand it. And they won't always support you in it.

The writer of Proverbs knew that. (And I'm pretty sure God knows that too.) That's why Proverbs 3:3 tells us to do whatever we've got to do to keep the faith. Tie it around your neck. Write it on your heart. Put it in your pocket. Print it on your T-shirt. But whatever you do, never, ever, ever let your faith leave you.

Faith takes work, but it's always worth it. Keep it close. You never know when you'll need it most.

Tell me about it
Has anyone ever disagreed with your faith?

Think about it
What are some things you can do when that happens?

DO IT!
Create a keepsake—a drawing, a Bible verse, or any little token—to remind you of your faith. Take it with you wherever you go.

God's Delight

Lying lips are detestable to the Lord, but faithful people are His delight.

—Proverbs 12:22

Did you know that you're a delight to the Lord? Yes, you. Little ol' you.

Your faithfulness makes God happy. Your worship makes Him smile. When you love Him and serve Him and tell people about Him, you bring joy to the Creator of the universe.

So when you're feeling small, when you think nothing you do matters at all, remember that God sees you. He loves you. And He delights in your faithfulness.

 Tell me about it
Name some ways that you have made God happy today.

💡 **Think about it**
Why do you think our faithfulness makes Him happy?

Draw a sad face and a happy face on a piece of paper. Under the sad face, list things that you think make God sad. Under the happy face, put things that make Him happy.

Blessed

A faithful man will have many blessings.

—Proverbs 28:20

We've learned a lot about being faithful so far. And by this point, Proverbs 28:20 is probably no surprise.

After all, we know that God is always with the faithful (Psalm 37:28). We know that our faithfulness makes God happy (Proverbs 12:22). And we know that God rewards those who try to find Him (Hebrews 11:6).

The message of Proverbs 28:20 is one the Bible shows us again and again. God wants us always to remember that He cares for the faithful. And although the faithful will face tough times, in the end, their lives will be blessed.

Knowing that this verse is true, how will you choose to live today and every day?

📣 Tell me about it

How is the message of Proverbs 28:20 true in your own life?

💡 Think about it

Can you think of other people you know or people in the Bible whose lives were blessed because of their faithfulness?

✋ DO IT!

Draw or make a list of your many blessings. Write Proverbs 28:20 at the top.

Stand Firm

"If you do not stand firm in your faith, then you will not stand at all."

—Isaiah 7:9

If you were building a big tower of blocks, would you build it on the floor? Or in a big bowl of Jell-O? Umm, the floor, right? Why? Because it's a firm foundation!

It's the same when you're building your life. You want to build it on something strong, steady, and everlasting—like a strong, steady, everlasting God. If you don't, Isaiah tells us, "you will not stand at all."

When you place your faith in stuff or even people, things can get wobbly. Stuff doesn't last very long, and people just aren't perfect. But when you place your faith in God, you know you've got a firm foundation to build a life on.

📢 Tell me about it
What are some things, besides God, that you place your faith in?

💡 Think about it
Why is God the best foundation to build your life on?

✋ DO IT!
Get out some blocks and try building towers in different places and on different foundations. Which works best? Why?

Live by Faith

The righteous one will live by his faith.
—Habakkuk 2:4

Sometimes the difference between right and wrong can get a bit fuzzy. Is it wrong to tell Mom that dinner was good—when it was really kind of gross? I'm not sure I can answer that. . . .

But the Bible does give us a lot of clear-cut answers about right and wrong. Just take a look at the Ten Commandments (Exodus 20:1–17). Or listen to Jesus talk about the greatest commandments (Mark 12:28–31). And one more answer is right here in Habakkuk: live by faith.

We've talked a lot about living by faith—how to do it and what it looks like in your life. And Habakkuk reminds us that every time you take a step of faith, it's a step in the right direction.

📣 Tell me about it

In your own words, what does righteous mean? (Ask your parents if you need help!)

💡 Think about it

Why do you think God wants us to be righteous?

✋ DO IT!

Write the word righteous in the middle of a piece of paper. Now, in all different colors, write as many words as you can think of that describe a person who is righteous.

The disciples were getting the hang of this faith thing. They had walked with Jesus as He preached. They had seen the many miracles He performed.

But then came the storm.

Jesus and His disciples were all in a boat, crossing the Sea of Galilee, when the wind started whipping and the waves started crashing. All they could see were the flashes of lightning and the driving rain. They couldn't hear over the thunder and the wind. But they could feel the water rushing around their feet—and rising. Where was Jesus?!?

They found Him—sleeping peacefully—at the back of the boat. "Jesus!" the grown men cried. "We're all going to die!!!"

Jesus opened His eyes and answered with an unexpected question: "Why are you afraid, you of little faith?" Then He turned to the storm. "Shh. Be quiet. Be still." And the wind and the waves obeyed.

It's pretty easy to keep our faith when the sun is shining and all is well. But the true test of our faith is when the scary days come. That's when we need to remember that Jesus is in control. He can even calm the storms.

Tell me about it

When is the last time something scary or stormy happened in your life?

💡 Think about it

Would Jesus have said you had big faith or little faith during that time?

DO IT!

On a piece of paper, draw the stormy scene from above. Then write the words from Matthew 8:27: "Even the winds and the sea obey Him!"

Faith You Can See

Seeing their faith, Jesus told the paralytic, "Have courage, son, your sins are forgiven."

—Matthew 9:2

Not everyone had "little faith" like the disciples in the storm. Sometimes people would step up and show Jesus big faith.

One man had heard of Jesus' healing power, but he couldn't go to see Him because he was paralyzed. Day and night, the man just lay there on a mat on the ground. But when the man's friends heard that Jesus was coming to town, they picked up the man— mat and all—and carried him to see Jesus.

When Jesus saw their great faith, He told the paralyzed man, "Get up, pick up your mat, and go home" (Matthew 9:6). Because this man and his friends had stepped out in big faith, Jesus quickly healed him and sent him on his way.

Tell me about it

When was a time that Jesus would have noticed your big faith?

Think about it

What is something that you would take to Jesus if you knew He could make it better?

DO IT!

What is that one thing that you need to have big faith about? Take it to Jesus right now, and trust Him to take care of you.

"Why did you Doubt?"

Immediately Jesus reached out His hand, caught hold of him, and said to him, "You of little faith, why did you doubt?"

—Matthew 14:31

The disciples were out on the water again when they saw a figure walking toward them on the sea. "It's a ghost!" they cried. But the voice answered, "Don't be afraid. It's Me, Jesus."

"Lord, if it's You," Peter tested, "let me walk to You on the water."

"Okay, come," the voice answered.

So Peter, in big faith, climbed out of the boat. And to everyone's surprise, he started walking out to Jesus on the sea! But then Peter noticed the howling wind. It scared him, and he began to sink. "Save me!" he cried to Jesus. And the steady hand of Jesus pulled Peter up.

Peter had stepped out in big faith. Then he lost it when things got scary. But you know the best part? Jesus was there to catch Peter, even when he lost his faith. And Jesus will catch you too.

Tell me about it
Was there ever a time when you got scared and were filled with doubt?

Think about it
Did you call to Jesus for help? What happened?

DO IT!
Fill a bowl with water. Try placing different items (like a paper clip, a penny, a leaf) on top of the water to see if they float.

Do you know how tiny a mustard seed is? It's a lot smaller than a watermelon seed or a sunflower seed. If you held one, it would just be a little dot in the middle of your hand.

But Jesus tells us that this is all we need—faith that big, the size of a mustard seed.

Do you ever feel like you have mountains to move? Do you have problems so big that you don't know how you'll get around them? Or do you have dreams so huge that you don't know how you'll ever reach them?

You just need a little faith. Tiny faith, even. Jesus said even with that, "Nothing will be impossible for you."

Tell me about it
What is one problem you need help with?

Think about it
What do you dream of doing one day?

DO IT!
Talk to Jesus right now about both of those things. And have a little mustard-seed faith that He will help you with your problems, your dreams, and everything in between.

Faithful over a Few

"You were faithful over a few things; I will put you in charge of many things."

—Matthew 25:23

When you brush your teeth, are you careful to clean every one? Or do you quickly run the toothbrush under the water without ever touching your teeth? When you clean your room, do you put everything neatly in its place? Or kick everything under the bed?

We can tell ourselves that these little things don't matter. We may try to skimp on the things that we think no one will notice. But Jesus tells us in Matthew that these things matter too. And they don't just matter; they prepare us for bigger things. If we do a good job on the little things, we'll get even bigger things to be in charge of.

Even if there were no reward, no bigger prizes waiting, we should work in a way that would make God proud. "In all the work you are doing, work the best you can. Work as if you were doing it for the Lord" (Colossians 3:23 ncv). And when we do, when we are faithful with the little things, big things will come our way.

Tell me about it
What is one little job that you don't like doing?

Think about it
Do you try your best on that job? Why or why not?

DO IT!
Make a list of chores to do around the house. At the bottom, in colorful letters, write the words of Colossians 3:23.

Grow Our Faith

The apostles said to the Lord, "Increase our faith."

—Luke 17:5

When being faithful with the little things is hard . . . when you don't even have a speck-of-dirt-size faith . . . where do you go? What do you do?

Well, the disciples went to Jesus, and they just asked, "Lord, increase our faith." They had seen Him heal the sick, help blind men to see, and feed thousands of people with a little boy's lunch. But they were still having trouble. As much as their faith had grown, they still needed more.

"Increase our faith." Make it grow. And you know what? I believe Jesus did just that.

He's been here on this earth, He knows it's tough, and He's here to help.

All we have to do is ask.

Tell me about it
When has your faith been the strongest?

Think about it
When was a time that your faith was weak?

DO IT!
Ask Jesus now to grow your faith. And just by knowing He will, your faith will already begin to grow.

Forgiveness by Faith

"By faith in Me they may receive forgiveness of sins."

—Acts 26:18

Maybe the best, most important part of our faith comes down to this: forgiveness.

John 3:16 tells us about God's perfect plan to forgive us: "For God loved the world in this way: He gave His One and Only Son, so that everyone who believes in Him will not perish but have eternal life."

Everybody messes up. None of us can be perfect. But Jesus, God's Son and the only perfect person to ever walk the earth, took all of our sins for us. When we believe in Him and ask Him to forgive us, He does. And our sins no longer get in the way of our relationship with a holy God. We can be close to Him, talk to Him, and know Him.

All of this is possible with faith. Our sins can be forgiven by a holy God who loves us so much that He gave the life of His only Son to make ours better.

Tell me about it
Why does God care if we sin?

Think about it
How does Jesus make forgiveness possible?

DO IT!
Talk to God about your sins and your need for forgiveness. And thank Him for making a way for us to have forgiveness through faith.

Stand by Faith

They were broken off by unbelief, but you stand by faith.

—Romans 11:20

Today's verse is only once sentence, but it says so much about faith. There's a clear difference in the two groups of people: *they* and *you*.

They didn't believe. They were broken off. You have faith. You stand strong.

As complicated as faith may seem sometimes, it really can be this simple. Do you have faith or don't you? Do you believe or do you not? Are you a *you* or are you a *they*?

The good news is: no one is beyond God's reach. God will add the *theys* to the *yous* if they choose to believe.

And together we can all stand strong in faith.

 Tell me about it
Why do you choose to believe?

💡 Think about it
Think of someone who may not believe yet. How could you help him or her see why you believe?

✋ DO IT!
Make a card, sing a song, or draw a picture for someone who does not believe yet. Ask God to show you how you can help him find his way to believe.

Faith can be a tough concept to grasp. We can't see it. We can't touch it. And we don't always understand it.

But I love the way it is described in 1 John 5:4. It's so real, so powerful; you can almost see it.

In the end, faith wins. Our God and our faith in Him are ultimately victorious over all the evil in this world. And to me, that makes it all worth it.

Stand strong in your faith. It truly will conquer the world.

📣 Tell me about it

How can faith conquer anything, especially the world?

💡 Think about it

What are some ways—today and every day—that you can fight the bad of this world with your faith?

DO IT!

What does our world look like when it is conquered by faith? Draw a picture or write a short story about it.

Faith and Hope

Now faith is the reality of what is hoped for.

—Hebrews 11:1

For more than thirty days now, we've learned about faith, talked about faith, and grown in faith.

Faith and hope go hand in hand. Faith is knowing that everything we hope for is real. Faith is knowing that hope isn't just a bubble that will pop and disappear. Faith is knowing that hope will come true—so true, you can hold it in your hands.

Faith and *hope* may be difficult for us to take hold of, but the Bible tells us that these things—faith, hope, and love—are the three things that last forever

(1 Corinthians 13:13). And since they'll be around forever, well, we might as well get to know them better.

📣 Tell me about it

In everything you've learned about faith so far, what is the one thing you remember the most?

💡 Think about it

How do faith and hope work together?

✋ DO IT!

On a piece of paper, in big letters, write your favorite verse about faith. Decorate it, draw a border around it, color it, and hang it where you will see it every day.

Walking Together Press is a non-profit publishing company devoted to supporting grassroots libraries in Africa through global book sales and through providing free library editions. To read our story, to see our catalog, and to learn more about how you can help us in our mission, visit our website at:

walkingtogether.press

Milton Keynes UK
Ingram Content Group UK Ltd.
UKHW050427081024
449408UK00003B/23